Series 536

BRITISH WILD FLOWERS

by
BRIAN VESEY-FITZGERALD, F.L.S.
with illustrations by
ROWLAND and EDITH HILDER

Publishers: Ladybird Books Ltd . Loughborough
© Ladybird Books Ltd (formerly Wills & Hepworth Ltd) 1957
Printed in England

Primrose The stem is stout, but grows underground and is not seen. The oval, rather wrinkled leaves grow in a rosette and usually lie flat to the ground. Their underside is softly hairy. The large pale creamy-yellow flowers are solitary, growing one on each stalk. They first appear in March and may be seen from then until the end of May. The Primrose is a common and beautiful flower in woods and hedgerows throughout Britain.

Sweet Violet The leaves and the shoots spring from a woody stock, which does not appear above ground. The leaves are heart-shaped and slightly hairy, and have long stalks. They grow bigger after the plant has flowered. The flowers are usually violet, but may be white with purple veins. Both types are sweetly scented and appear in March and April. The Sweet Violet is a common plant of hedgerows and woods in southern England.

Wood Anemone Also known as the " Windflower," because it is never still. There is no visible stem. Both leaves and flowers have long slender stalks, and the flowers are solitary, one to a stalk. The flowers are white or very pale purple, grow to a height of about six inches, and appear from March until May. The Wood Anemone grows in colonies, and is common in woods throughout Britain.

1 *Primrose*
2 *Sweet Violet*
3 *Wood Anemone*

4

0 7214 0093 0

Early Purple Orchis One of the easiest of the Orchid family to find, since it is common in pastures and open woods throughout Britain. But it should be remembered that the leaves are not always spotted as they are in the picture. The flowers appear from April to June. The Early Purple Orchis can be distinguished from the Spotted Orchis, which is also common and grows in the same sort of country at the same time, by the open spike. The spike of the Spotted Orchis is dense (the flowers very close together) and shaped like a pyramid, and the leaves are always spotted.

Cuckoo-Pint There are many different country names for this plant. You may know it as " Lords-and-Ladies " or " Jack-in-the-Pulpit " or " Wild Arum." The flower, which is a green hood shielding a purple club or spike, appears before the leaves and may be seen at any time from April to June. The leaves are dark glossy green and often spotted. The scarlet berries, which appear in the autumn, are *poisonous*. The Cuckoo-Pint is a common plant of hedgerows.

Wood Sorrel Hardly ever grows to a greater height than three inches. The white flowers are sometimes tinged with lilac, and are solitary; that is, there is only one flower on each slender stalk. They close up shortly after sunset, and are then almost impossible to see. The Wood Sorrel flowers from April to June, and is very common in woods throughout Britain.

1 *Early Purple Orchis*
2 *Cuckoo-Pint*   3 *Wood Sorrel*

6

Stinking Hellebore   Sometimes called the
" Setterwort."   The stem is stout and grows to a foot,
or a little more, in height.   The flowers are green, and
appear from the middle of February to early April.
The Stinking Hellebore can be distinguished from the
Green Hellebore (or Bear's-foot), which also has
green flowers, by the sepals (the outer leaves of the bud)
which are tinged at the edge with purple.   The
Stinking Hellebore is a very rare plant of stony places
in southern England.

Snowdrop   Everyone knows the Snowdrop because it is often planted in gardens, where it flowers
in the winter and sometimes even at Christmas.   In
the wild plant the white, drooping flowers do not
appear until February, and may be seen from then
until the end of March.   It grows in copses and thin
woods, and as a wild plant is very far from common.

1 *Stinking Hellebore*
2 *Snowdrop*

Ground Ivy This is no relation to the common Ivy, but a cousin of the catmint of our gardens. The branching stem trails along the ground, and the heart-shaped leaves are carried on long stalks. The flowering stems are more or less erect, and the bright purple-blue flowers appear from March to June. It is a common plant of shady places.

Bluebell This is a member of the Lily family. The glossy leaves are strap-shaped, and the blue, bell-shaped flowers are drooping. The bluebell seeds profusely and also multiplies by offshoots from its bulbs, so it usually occurs in masses. It is very common in woods and along shady banks from April to June.

Red Campion A tall plant, growing up to two feet. The leaves at the base are oval and have long stalks, but those on the stem are short-stalked, more pointed and hairy. The deep rose-coloured flowers are about one inch across, and appear from April to October. This is a very common plant of shady hedgerows.

1 Ground Ivy
2 Bluebell
3 Red Campion

Marsh Marigold This is the proper name for the flower that almost everybody calls the " King-cup." It grows to a height of a foot to eighteen inches, and has smooth shiny leaves. The flowers are large and a beautiful golden-yellow. They first appear in early March and may be seen at any time from then until the end of June. The Marsh Marigold is very common in damp meadows and marshes.

Lady's Smock Often called the " Cuckooflower," because it is supposed to flower on the day when the cuckoo is first heard. As a matter of fact, it does appear at very much the same time. The stem is erect and the flowers are lilac. They may be seen from mid-April until the end of June. It is a very common plant of damp meadows, shady lanes and streamsides.

Butterbur This is a plant of riverbanks, and it flowers in March and April. It has large, heart-shaped leaves, which are covered with cobwebby hairs on the underside. The flowers are pinkish-purple, and individually quite small, but the whole plant may be as much as a yard across. It is a common plant of riverbanks and streamsides.

1 Marsh Marigold
2 Lady's Smock
3 Butterbur

Yellow Flag The Yellow Iris. The brilliant yellow flowers normally grow taller than the stiff leaves, and may be seen at any time from early May until the end of August. The seeds are pale brown. It grows only in damp places, and is very common in marshes and along the banks of rivers and streams, lakes and ponds.

Meadow Sweet Sometimes called the " Queen of the Meadows." A tall, erect plant, growing to about three feet in height. The stem is reddish, stiff and furrowed. The small, creamy-white flowers have a sweet scent, and may be seen from early June to late September. It is very common in meadows and along roadsides.

Forget-Me-Not The flowers are bright blue with a yellow eye, and the petals are slightly notched. They may be seen at any time between early June and the end of August. The Forget-Me-Not is a common plant of damp, shady places, especially ditches, throughout Britain.

1 *Yellow Flag*
2 *Meadow Sweet*
3 *Forget-Me-Not*

Purple Loosestrife The erect stem grows to a height of three feet. The rather hairy leaves grow in pairs or threes up the stem. The reddish-purple flowers appear from July to September in showy spikes. A common plant of marshy places and riverbanks.

Water Avens There are large leaves at ground level and small hairy leaflets grow up the stem, which is erect and may reach two feet. The drooping purplish flowers appear from May to July. A common plant of damp, shady places throughout Britain.

Greater Stitchwort The stem is very slender and weak at the base, but thickens and has four distinct angles further up. The rich green leaves are lance-shaped and rough and the white flowers appear from April to June. A common plant in hedgebanks and woods.

1 *Purple Loosestrife*
2 *Water Avens*
3 *Greater Stitchwort*

Corn Marigold The stem is erect with spreading branches, and the smooth, bluish-green, rather fleshy leaves are scented. The beautiful, large, rich yellow flowers may be seen at any time from June to September. This is a common weed of cornfields throughout Britain.

Corn Mint Also known as Field Mint. The stem is very branched and spreading, and grows from six inches to a foot in height. The oval leaves grow in pairs, one leaf opposite the other, up the stem. The pale purple flowers appear at the junction of the opposite leaves, and may be seen from July to September. A common plant of cornfields and waste places.

Hemlock Water Dropwort A coarse branching plant, growing up to three feet in height. The leaves are large and fern-like, and the white flowers are carried in large spreading groups at the ends of the stems. They may be seen from June until the end of August. A *very poisonous* plant, which is very common in ditches.

Feverfew Also known as Scentless Mayweed. The stem is very branched and the leaves are deeply notched. The white, daisy-like flowers have solid yellow centres and may be seen from July to September. A common plant of cornfields and waste places.

1 *Corn Marigold*
2 *Corn Mint*
3 *Hemlock Water Dropwort*
4 *Feverfew*

18

Honeysuckle Also known as Woodbine. A woody, climbing plant with slightly hairy leaves. The sweetly-scented flowers appear from June to July, and are white or cream, tinged with yellow and red. The berries are crimson. It is common in hedges and woods throughout Britain.

Ivy An evergreen shrub which climbs by means of roots on the stem. The leaves are long-stalked, leathery and glossy. The small yellowish-green flowers appear from September to November. The berries are black, and are *poisonous* to humans, but not to birds. Very common on walls and banks and on trees everywhere.

Greater Bindweed A weak-stemmed climber, which twines round more or less upright supports. The large white, funnel-shaped flowers appear from June to October. Very common in hedges and as a garden weed.

White Bryony A climber with long branching stems and five-pointed hairy leaves. The small yellowish flowers appear from May to July. The berries are red. A fairly common plant in hedges in southern England.

1 *Honeysuckle*
2 *Ivy*
3 *Greater Bindweed*
4 *White Bryony*

Dog Rose   The most common of our wild roses. It can be distinguished from the Sweetbriar, which is also very common, by the underside of the leaves. The Sweetbriar has red sticky glands on the underside of its leaves : the Dog Rose has not.   The flowers of the Dog Rose may be either pink or white, and are scented.   They usually come in the first week of June, and may be seen from then until the middle of July.   It is a very common plant of hedgerows.

Foxglove   A tall plant, growing from two to five feet in height.   The large leaves grow alternately up the stem, and the long flowers are bell-shaped and usually reddish-purple spotted with white.   They may be seen from June until September.   This is a *poisonous* plant.   It is common in fields, heaths, and open woods, except on chalk soils.

White Campion   A plant with an erect stem, growing to about two feet in height, with soft hairy leaves.   The white flowers open in the evening and are very popular with moths.   They may be seen at any time from the middle of May until the end of September. White Campion is common along hedgebanks and in waste places.

1 *Dog Rose*
2 *Foxglove*
3 *White Campion*

Periwinkle The stem is trailing and branching. The dark green, shining leaves are evergreen. The flowering stems are short and erect, and the bright blue flowers grow singly on short stalks. They may be seen from March to June. A fairly common plant of woods and shady hedgerows.

Toothwort This is a brown parasitic plant, which grows on the roots of trees. The stem is fleshy and white. The pale lilac flowers may grow to a height of a foot. They appear in April and May. This is not at all a common plant.

1 *Periwinkle*
2 *Toothwort*

Musk Mallow The stem branches from the base, each branch carrying a single flower. The leaves on the stem are deeply cut, but those at ground level are not. The large pale rose flowers appear from June to September. This is a fairly common plant of waysides and especially of railway embankments.

Agrimony The erect stem grows to a height of about eighteen inches. The leaves are stalked and hairy, and there are small leaflets between the larger leaves. The small yellow flowers are borne in long spikes from June to October. A common plant of meadows and waysides.

Betony The stem is erect and hairy, and grows to about two feet. The leaves are oblong and have blunt teeth. The purple flowers appear in a dense spike from June to August. A common plant of woods and rough pastures.

Wall Pennywort A small plant, usually about four inches high. The leaves are fleshy and circular. The small creamy-green flowers droop on erect stems, and may be seen from June to August. This is a fairly common plant of stone walls and rocky banks.

1 *Musk Mallow*
2 *Agrimony*
3 *Betony*
4 *Wall Pennywort*

Rosebay Willow-Herb Also known as "Fireweed" and "French Willow." A tall plant, growing up to five feet in height. The flowers, which appear in late July and August, are rosy purple and have petals of unequal lengths. This plant may be found in great numbers where trees have been felled and on bombed sites in cities, but it is common in open woods and copses everywhere.

Ragwort The stem is erect and very tough. It grows to a height of two or three feet, branching out towards the top. The large, bright yellow flowers may be seen from July to the end of September. Though beautiful to look at from a distance, this is one of the most troublesome weeds of agricultural land. It is very common along waysides and on poor pastures.

Beaked Parsley The leaves are large and fern-like with many finely-pointed leaflets. The stem is erect, furrowed, and branches out towards the top. The white flowers appear in May and June. One of the commonest plants of hedgerows.

1 *Rosebay Willow-Herb*
2 *Ragwort*
3 *Beaked Parsley*

Heartsease Also known as the Field Pansy. This is a very variable plant. It may grow anything from two inches to a foot in height, and the flowers may be yellow, purple, purple-and-yellow, or white. They may be seen from May to September. A common plant in fields.

Self-Heal The stem branches and spreads from its base, and rarely grows to a greater height than six inches. The leaves are hairy. The blue-purple flowers grow in dense spikes, and appear in June and July. A very common plant of grassy places throughout Britain.

Greater Celandine The leaves are long, thin, and cut into deep segments. They are green on one side and pale bluish-grey on the other. The stem is full of *poisonous* yellow juice. The small yellow flowers appear from May to August. A common plant of shady places and old walls.

Silverweed The leaves are silvery and hairy underneath. The bright yellow flowers, which are nearly an inch across, are solitary and carried on long stalks. They appear from May to August. This is a common plant of waste places and roadsides, and may also be found on shingle beaches.

1 *Heartsease*
2 *Self-Heal*
3 *Greater Celandine*
4 *Silverweed*

Viper's Bugloss One of the most handsome of all British wildflowers. A tall erect plant with a stout stem, growing to a height of three feet, it is covered with stiff hairs. The large, irregular, bright blue flowers appear from June to August. It is found only in dry places, mostly in southern England.

Yellow Toadflax The stem is stiff and erect, growing to a height of about eighteen inches. There are many long, narrow leaves. The yellow flowers appear from July to October and have orange mouths. A common plant of roadsides and cornfields.

Bee Orchis The few pink and brown flowers grow in a loose spike. The lip is as broad as long, velvet brown with yellow markings, and puffed out, so that it looks like a bee settled on the flower. The flowers may be seen in June and July on chalk soils in southern England. It is not common.

Butterfly Orchis The large white, sweetly scented flowers, grow in a loose graceful spike. There is no particular resemblance to a butterfly, and the plant is chiefly visited by moths. The flowers may be seen from June to August in moist fields and woods. A fairly common plant.

1 *Viper's Bugloss*
2 *Yellow Toadflax*
3 *Bee Orchis*
4 *Butterfly Orchis*

32

Rest Harrow This is a shrub, which may grow as high as two feet. It has no real stem, but many low spreading branches and oval leaves with small sharp teeth. The whole plant is covered with soft, rather sticky hairs and has an unpleasant smell. The lovely, rose-pink flowers appear from July to September. A common plant of sandy places, especially near the sea.

Cross-Leaved Heath A small woody plant with slender, erect, branching stems and narrow, greyish leaves, which are arranged in groups of four. The large, pink flowers are in drooping clusters, and appear from June to September. This is a very common shrub on moist heaths throughout Britain.

Ling This is the plant which is usually called Heather or Scottish Heather. It is a shrub which may grow to anything between six inches and three feet in height, with many branching erect stems. The leaves are three-cornered and very small and numerous. The pink or white flowers, which appear from July to September, are also very small and are arranged in dense spikes. This is a very common plant on heaths and moors throughout Britain.

Harebell A plant which grows to about a foot in height on a wiry, erect stem. The lower leaves are heart-shaped and have long stalks, but they disappear before the flowers come. The small flowers may be seen from July to September. They are pale blue and drooping on long stalks. A common plant of heaths and pastures throughout Britain.

1 Rest Harrow   3 Ling
2 Cross-Leaved Heath 4 Harebell

Poppy   The flower in the picture is the common Red Poppy, also known as the Corn Poppy and the Corn Rose. The stem is branched with many bristly hairs, and grows to a height of about two feet. The flowers may be as much as three inches across, and one pair of petals is always much larger than the other. At seeding time the seeds are jerked a considerable distance, so the Poppy often appears in unexpected places. Common in cornfields and waste places, the flowers may be seen from June to August.

Bladder Campion   Also known as White Bottle. An erect branching plant, which is very similar to the White Campion, but has rather broader leaves with a whitish bloom on them. The flowers, which may be seen from late May to early September, often open a little earlier in the day than those of the White Campion and are also very popular with moths. Common in cornfields, along roadsides and in waste places.

1 *Poppy*
2 *Bladder Campion*

Tansy A tall plant, two to three feet in height. The ridged stem is tough and erect. The smooth. dark green leaves are scented. The yellow flowers are small and rather like buttons, and appear from July to December. This is a common plant of waste places throughout Britain.

Succory Also known as Chicory. A tall plant, one to three feet in height, with an erect, branching stem. The leaves are hairy and clasp the stem. The bright blue flowers appear from July to September, and are about one-and-a-half inches across. They wither after one day. The roasted roots of this plant are used as a substitute for coffee. This plant is not uncommon in dry fields and waysides.

1 Tansy
2 Succory

Jack-By-The-Hedge Also known as Garlic Mustard and Sauce Alone. A coarse, erect, very leafy plant, growing to a height of three feet. The dark green leaves are large, broad, and heart-shaped. They smell of garlic when rubbed. The white flowers appear from April to June. This is one of the commonest plants of hedgebanks.

Cowslip Also known as Paigle. The stem has a stout stock, and the wrinkled leaves are at ground level. The flowers are borne on a long stalk, which may grow to a height of eight inches. They are deep yellow with orange spots, and appear from April to June. This is a common plant of meadow land.

Daisy The stock is branching, and the leaves, which are spoon-shaped, grow in the form of a rosette. The white flowers grow singly on naked stalks. They close at sunset and may be seen in every month of the year. This is by far the most common British wildflower.

1 Jack-By-The-Hedge
2 Cowslip
3 Daisy

40

White Dead-Nettle   This is not the stinging nettle, and is called the "dead" nettle because it does not sting. It grows in dense clumps with erect, unbranched stems reaching to two feet. It can be distinguished from the stinging nettle by its flowers, which are white : those of the stinging nettle are green. The flowers may be seen from March to October, much earlier and much later than the stinging nettle. A common plant of waysides.

Buttercup   There are several sorts of Buttercup, all very much alike.   The one in the picture is the common Field Buttercup, which may grow as high as two feet and has hairy leaves. The large, bright yellow flowers appear from May until October. Very common in meadows throughout Britain.

Meadow Crane's-Bill   This is a most striking plant, for it grows to a height of two to three feet and the large, purple-blue flowers, which always grow in pairs, are an inch or more across. The flowers appear in June, July and August. A common plant in meadows and along roadsides.

1 *White Dead-Nettle*
2 *Buttercup*
3 *Meadow Crane's-Bill*

Knapweed The tough, erect stem grows to a height of about two feet. The dark green leaves are lance-shaped and hairy. The reddish-purple flowers are about an inch across and hard to the touch. Knapweed is in flower from June to September, and is common in meadows and along waysides.

St. John's Wort There are many flowers in this family, all rather alike and not at all easy to tell apart. But you can tell the common St. John's Wort because the oblong leaves have clear transparent dots on them. The yellow flowers appear from July to September, and are very common in meadows and dry places.

Bird's-Foot Trefoil The stem is very branched and spread out on the ground. But the orange-yellow flowers are carried on long erect stalks. The plant is in flower right through the summer from early May to late September. It gets its name from the long dark-brown seed pods, which spread out like a bird's foot. One of the most common of all British wildflowers.

1 Knapweed
2 St. John's Wort
3 Bird's-Foot Trefoil

Comfrey A large, stout plant, growing up to three feet in height, with branching stems and large lance-shaped leaves. The flowers are very variable in colour : dull purple is, perhaps, the most common, but they may be yellow or dirty white. They first appear in May, and may be seen from then until the end of July. This is a common plant of damp meadows and shady waysides.

Common Vetch The Common Vetch belongs to the same family as the Broad Bean of our kitchen gardens and allotments. It has a narrow, smooth pod, which is very like the Broad Bean pod. Inside there are ten to twelve seeds, which look very like small broad beans. The flowers are large and reddish purple. This is one of the most common plants of fields and waysides.

Germander Speedwell The stem of this plant runs along the ground, but the branches, which bear the flowers, are erect. The leaves are heart-shaped and hairy and the flowers bright blue. They first appear in April and may be seen from then until the end of June. The flowers never open on a cold day. This is a common plant of hedgebanks and open woods.

1 *Comfrey*
2 *Common Vetch*
3 *Germander Speedwell*

Common Mallow Quite unmistakable with its stout, erect stem and its large, rough, long-stalked leaves. The reddish-purple flowers are big too ; often nearly two inches across. They first appear in early June and may be seen from then until the end of October. It is a very common plant of roadsides and waste places.

Horned Poppy Also known as the " Sea Poppy." The stem is stout and branched, and grows to a height of between one and two feet. The large yellow flowers are carried on very short stalks and may be seen from June to the end of September. The seed pods are very long (sometimes twelve inches) narrow and curved. The Horned Poppy grows only on sandy and shingle beaches, and is not at all common.

Lesser Bindweed The stem is weak and trailing or twining. Unlike the Greater Bindweed, which is a great climber of hedges and fences and a common garden weed, the Lesser Bindweed rarely gets more than two feet off the ground. The flowers, which appear from early June to late September, may be either white or pink. Each flower lasts only for one day. It is common on banks and along waysides and, especially, in cornfields.

1 Common Mallow
2 Horned Poppy
3 Lesser Bindweed

Sea Holly   The stem is stout and erect, and the leaves are stiff and broad and very prickly. The flowers are bluish or bluish-purple, round and rather spiny : not unlike the flowers of the thistle. They appear towards the end of July and are rarely seen after the middle of August. The Sea Holly is quite common on sandy shores.

Samphire   A small, bushy plant with numerous branches spreading from a woody stock. The leaves are smooth, thick and fleshy, and are divided into narrow segments. When crushed they give off a pleasant scent. The greenish-white flowers are very small and are borne in umbels : that is, all the flower-stalks spring from one point. They first appear about midsummer and may be seen until the end of August. The Samphire grows on cliffs and rocks along the south and west coasts of England.

Scarlet Pimpernel   Also known as the "Poor-Man's-Weather-Glass." The stem branches from the base, and the branches spread out, but rarely rise to a height of more than six inches. The flowers are usually red, but may be pink, white or even blue, and have broad over-lapping petals. They close up at sunset and never open in cool weather. They first appear early in May and continue right through the summer to the end of September. The Scarlet Pimpernel is a very common weed of cornfields and gardens.

1 *Sea Holly*
2 *Samphire*
3 *Scarlet Pimpernel*

INDEX OF WILD FLOWERS